Improve Your Sight-reading!

A workbook for examinations

Flute Grade 6

PAUL HARRIS

FABER *ff* MUSIC

£6.50

NAME		

EXAMINATION RECORD

Grade	Date	Mark

TEACHER'S NAME
TELEPHONE

© 1997 by Faber Music Ltd
First published in 1997 by Faber Music Ltd
Bloomsbury House 74–77 Great Russell Street London WC1B 3DA
Music and text set by Silverfen
Cover illustration by Drew Hillier
Printed in England by Caligraving Ltd
All rights reserved

ISBN10: 0-571-51789-7
EAN13: 978-0-571-51789-3

To buy Faber Music publications or to find out about the full range of titles available
please contact your local music retailer or Faber Music sales enquiries:

Faber Music Limited, Burnt Mill, Elizabeth Way, Harlow, CM20 2HX England
Tel: +44 (0)1279 82 89 82   Fax: +44 (0)1279 82 89 83
sales@fabermusic.com   fabermusic.com

INTRODUCTION

The ability to sight-read fluently is an essential part of your training as a musician, whether you intend to play professionally, or simply for enjoyment. Yet the *study* of sight-reading is often badly neglected by young players and is frequently regarded as no more than an unpleasant side-line. If you become a good sight-reader you will be able to learn pieces more quickly, play in ensembles and orchestras with confidence and earn extra marks in grade exams!

Using the workbook

The purpose of this workbook is to incorporate sight-reading regularly into your practice and lessons, and to help you prepare for the sight-reading test in grade examinations. It offers you a progressive series of enjoyable and stimulating stages in which, with careful work, you should show considerable improvement from week to week.

Each stage consists of two parts: firstly, exercises which you should prepare in advance, along with a short piece with questions; and secondly, an unprepared test, to be found later in the book. At the top of the first page in each stage you will see one or two new features to be introduced. At the end there is a box for your assessment.

There are four different types of exercise:

1 **Rhythmic exercises** It is very important that you should be able to feel and maintain a steady pulse. These exercises will help you develop this ability. There are at least four ways of doing these exercises: clap or tap the lower line (the beat or pulse) while singing the upper line to 'la'; tap the lower line with your foot and clap the upper line; on a table or flat surface, tap the lower line with one hand and the upper line with the other; 'play' the lower line on a metronome and clap or tap the upper line.

2 **Melodic exercises** Fluent sight-reading depends on recognising melodic shapes at a glance. These shapes are often related to scales and arpeggios. Before you begin, always notice the *key-signature* and the notes affected by it, along with any accidentals.

3 **A prepared piece with questions** You should prepare carefully both the piece and the questions, which are to help you think about and understand the music before you play it.

4 **Unprepared piece** Finally your teacher will give you an *unprepared* test to be read at *sight*.

Remember to feel the pulse throughout each piece and to keep going at a steady and even tempo. Always try to look ahead, at least to the next note or beat.

Marking

Each stage carries 45 marks.

   15 marks for the rhythmic and melodic exercises
   15 marks for the combined questions and prepared test
   15 marks for the unprepared test (You should devise a similar series of questions for the unprepared test, and take the student's answers into account when allocating a final mark.)

Space is given at the end of each stage to maintain a running total so that progress may be clearly observed.

STAGE 1

Ab major
6
8

RHYTHMIC EXERCISES

1

2

3

MELODIC EXERCISES

1

mf

2

f

3

mp

4

p

PREPARED PIECE

1 In which key is this piece? Look through the piece and mentally note the D♭s.

2 Will you count 2 or 6 or a combination of the two?

3 Where might you make your first mistake?

4 What will determine your tempo?

5 How will you make the *dim. poco a poco* effective?

6 Study the first four bars for a few moments, then clap them from memory.

Total:

Unprepared tests page 18

Mark*:

Prepared work total:

Unprepared:

Total:

*The mark boxes are to be filled in by your teacher (see Introduction).

STAGE 2

Db major
More ties

RHYTHMIC EXERCISES

MELODIC EXERCISES

PREPARED PIECE

1   In which key is this piece? Look through the piece and mentally note the G♭s.

2   How many times does the rhythm of the first two bars reappear?

3   What will determine your tempo?

4   What do the lines above and beneath some notes indicate?

5   What pattern is the first phrase (bars 1–2) based on?

6   Study bars 9–12 for a few moments, then play them from memory.

Total:

Allegro moderato

Unprepared tests page 19

Mark:

Prepared work total:

Unprepared:

Total:

Running totals:

1   2

STAGE 3

B major
More rhythms in $\frac{5}{8}$

RHYTHMIC EXERCISES

1

2

3

MELODIC EXERCISES

1

2

3

4

5

PREPARED PIECE

1 In which key is this piece? Look through the piece and mentally note the A♯s.

2 How will you interpret the marking *Allegro deciso*?

3 How will you finger the D♯, B, C♯ in bars 5–6?

4 How will you interpret the markings in the first full bar?

5 Which part of the piece will be the loudest?

6 Study the first 4-bar phrase for a few moments, then clap it from memory.

Total:

Unprepared tests page 20

Mark:

Prepared work total:

Unprepared:

Total:

Running totals:

1	2	3

STAGE 4

C♯ minor
9
8

RHYTHMIC EXERCISES

MELODIC EXERCISES

PREPARED PIECE

1 In which key is this piece? Look through the piece and mentally note the B♯s.

2 Think through the fingering for the notes in bar 10.

3 How will you count this piece?

4 What is the musical purpose of the *poco rit.* and *a tempo* (bars 7–8)?

5 How will you achieve the *espressivo* effect?

6 Study the final 3 bars for a few moments, then clap them from memory.

Total:

Lento espressivo

mf

f   *dim.*

poco rit.   **a tempo**

mp

rall.

f

Unprepared tests page 21   Mark:

Prepared work total:

Unprepared:

Total:

Running totals:

1	2	3	4

STAGE 5

G♯ minor
rests

RHYTHMIC EXERCISES

MELODIC EXERCISES

PREPARED PIECE

1 In which key is this piece? What is its relative major?
   Look through the piece and mentally note the A♯s.

2 Think through the rhythm of the first 2 bars; now clap them from memory.

3 How many times does that rhythm occur?

4 What is the musical purpose of the *poco rit.* and *a tempo* (bars 6–7)?

5 Make a mental note of the fingering you will use for each F✗.

6 What character will you try to give to this piece?

Total:

Unprepared tests page 22

Mark:

Prepared work total:

Unprepared:

Total:

Running totals:

1	2	3	4	5

STAGE 6

RHYTHMIC EXERCISES

MELODIC EXERCISES

PREPARED PIECE

1　In which key is this piece?

2　In which note values will you count?

3　Study bars 5 and 6 for a moment; now play them from memory.

4　Where does the music of the opening return? How does it differ?

5　How will you achieve the character of *grazioso*?

6　In which bar might you make a *poco rit.* and why?

Total:

Unprepared tests page 23

Mark:

Prepared work total:

Unprepared:

Total:

Running totals:

1	2	3	4	5	6

STAGE 7

RHYTHMIC EXERCISES

MELODIC EXERCISES

PREPARED PIECE

1   In which style is this piece written?

2   Sing the piece through in your head.

3   What is the musical purpose of the first two bars?

4   Where does the first tune (bar 3) return? How does it differ?

5   Make a mental note of the A♯s and their fingerings.

6   Which will be the loudest part of the piece?

Total:

Gentle swing tempo

Unprepared tests page 24

Mark:

Prepared work total:

Unprepared:

Total:

Running totals:

1	2	3	4	5	6	7

UNPREPARED TESTS

STAGE 1

STAGE 2

STAGE 3

STAGE 4

STAGE 5

1 **Lento e serioso**

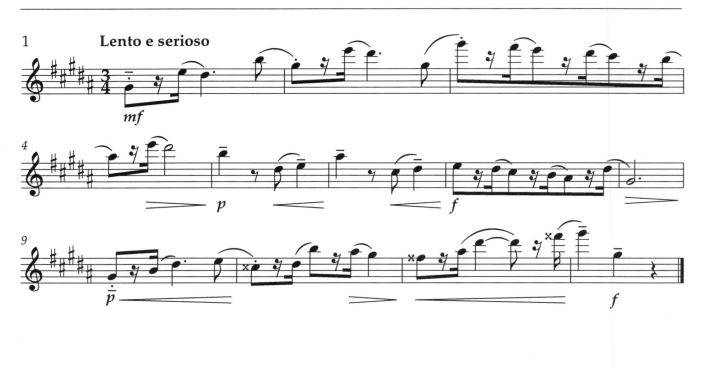

2 **Andante con moto**

3 **Dolce**

STAGE 6

STAGE 7